# It’s Me, Jeremiah

by

Jeremiah Jackson

It's Me, Jeremiah

by Jeremiah Jackson



Printed in the United States

Edited by Gerri Barnauskas

Illustrated by: Briana & Danielle Jackson

Edited, formatted, and published by

Destiny House Publishing, LLC.

P.O. Box 19774

Detroit, MI 48219

inquiry@destinyhousepublishing.com

www.destinyhousepublishing.com

404.993.0830

Cover by Kingdom Graphic Designs

ISBN: 978-1-936867-94-3

Table of Contents

# Chapter 1:

## It's Me, Jeremiah

Hello, my name is Jeremiah. But some people call me Jay or JJ. I am 9 years old. I live in the United States in Redford Michigan. I live in a house with my dad, mom and sisters, Briana and

Danielle. My favorite TV shows are *Pencilmation*, *Mr. Beast* and *Spongebob*.

I really like dogs. If I could choose a dog, it would be a Pomeranian, but I would want a puppy. I like Pomeranians because they are small and cute puppies. Sometimes when you look at them, they remind me of a little cat. If I had a Pomeranian, I would name it Rigby from *The Regular Show*. I would walk and feed Rigby every day and even teach him tricks. I would teach Rigby how to spin around and do flips. I've been asking my mom and dad for a dog, but they said no because I do not clean my room.

My favorite things to do when I am not in school is play with my friends, play video games and draw.

I like to draw characters like Sonic, Pencilmation, and Goku. My favorite 3 snacks are Doritos, cookies & cream ice cream, and homemade cornbread.

When I grow up, I want to drive a school bus and be a 3rd grade teacher. My plan is to get up early in the morning and drive my car to the school. I will then hop on the school bus to pick up the kids from the bus stop and then drive them to school. When I open the school bus door everyone will get off the bus and go to class. I will take the 3rd graders with me to my class to learn. Lastly, when school is over we will get back on my bus so that I can take everyone back to their bus stop. Then I will drive the bus back to the school and get in my car to go home.

I love to read books. The books that I read the most are chapter books and comedy books. My favorite chapter books are *Dogman, Captain Underpants*, *Judy Moody* and *Diary of a Wimpy Kid*. I want to be an author just like Dave Pilkey. But I want to be a child author and write lots of books.

What are your favorite things to do?

# Chapter 2:

## Calling All Friends

I have many friends. But Anthony and Amaya are my best friends. Anthony, Amaya, and I are in Mrs. Barnauskas' 3rd grade class at Vandenberg Elementary. Amaya and I ride the same bus to school. Sometimes Anthony, Amaya and I get to sit together at school. But most of the time we have to sit in our assigned seats. During recess we get to play with each other again. We went on field trips to the Detroit Zoo, bowling, the Capital in Lansing, and a Detroit Tiger's baseball game. We had lots of fun. After school, we call each other on the phone. We all play Roblox games online. Anthony, Amaya, and I hang out at my house sometimes. We jump on the trampoline, and play games like tag, basketball and have water balloon fights.

Anthony has been my friend from kindergarten. He is 9 years old. His birthday is in December, just like mine. Anthony's favorite foods are hamburgers and fries. His favorite color is blue. He likes karate. We go to the movies and bowling. We both play baseball, but we battle against each other.

My other best friend is Amaya. Amaya has been my friend from preschool. She is 9 years old. Her birthday is in April. Her favorite color is blue, the same as Anthony. Amaya's favorite thing to do is play with her dog, Cinnamon. She loves Paw Patrol. We went to see the movie Paw Patrol together.

When we went on the field trip to Lansing, I bought a dog from the gift shop. I named him Peanut Butter. Amaya and I decided to share Peanut Butter. She kept Peanut Butter on the weekend, and I kept him during the week. I took Peanut Butter on our trip to the zoo. But we lost Peanut Butter and could not find him. We were both sad. My mom is going to take me back to Lansing to the gift shop so that I can buy another dog for Amaya and I to share.

What do you like to do with your friends?

# Chapter 3:

## Surviving 3rd Grade

I am a 3rd grader at Vandenberg Elementary. I want to give you tips that I learned that helped me to survive the 3rd grade.

I ride the school bus to school every day.

**Tip #1:** You have to be at the bus stop early so you won't miss the bus!

At my school we have recess every day. At recess we play and have fun.

**Tip #2:** Always be safe and do not say bad words or do inappropriate things so that you don't miss recess.

Third grade math is easy and hard. Four-digit addition and subtraction were easy for me. But multiplication was kind of hard.

**Tip #3:** Watch lots of YouTube videos to learn the multiplication facts.

Bullies are really mean. They take stuff from you, say mean things about you, and sometimes hit you.

**Tip #4:** My teacher always tells us to tell her if something is wrong or if you're being bullied. But my dad and mom tell me that I have to defend myself if a bully is bothering me.

I have lots of friends in the 3rd grade. All of my friends are nice and we hang out a lot.

**Tip #5:** Never boss your friends around or they will not want to be friends with you.

There is a lot to learn in 3rd grade. We do math, science, social studies, and reading comprehension.

**Tip #6:** Always do your homework so that you can do better in school.

Do you have any tips to help students survive third grade?

# Chapter 4:

## Gaming!! Gaming!! Gaming!!

I love playing video games! It's my favorite thing to do when I'm not playing baseball or with my friends.

On the Xbox 360, I like to play Fortnite and Minecraft. My dad bought me 2 new games. They are Batman 2 and Major League Baseball

2K7. When I spend the night at my Auntie Arynn's house, we play Mortal Kombat together.

My favorite game to play on the Wii is the Michael Jackson Experience. I like to sing and dance to the music, but sometimes I can't keep up with the moves. I'm better at the Michael Jackson video now because I found Michael Jackson dance video on YouTube that I practice with. Michael Jackson is my favorite performer.

The game that I play the most is Roblox. I play with Amaya and my cousin, Amira. Both my sisters Bri and Danielle buy me Robux when I do good in school or after I'm done with my chores.

# What is your favorite game to play?

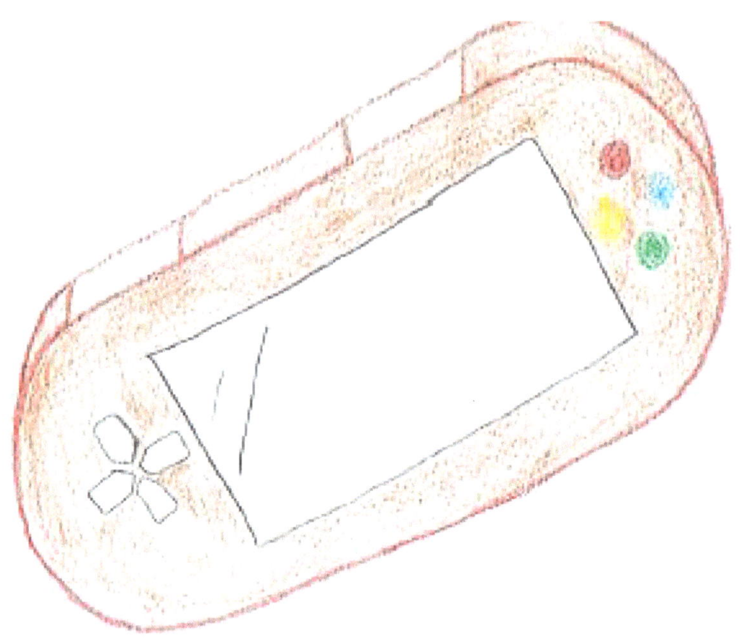

# Chapter 5:

## Sports Mania

I like watching and playing sports with my dad. My dad and I watch the NBA. My favorite basketball players are Michael Jordan, Kobe Bryant and Lebron James. My dad's favorite basketball player is Charles Barkley. Sometimes my dad and I play basketball together in the backyard.

On Sundays, my dad and I watch football. Our favorite football team is the Detroit Lions. Sometimes we play football in the backyard together with my friends. My mom and dad said they are going to put me in football next year.

My dad, my sister Danielle and I watch WWE. We watch Monday Night Raw and Friday Night Smackdown. My favorite WWE wrestlers are John Cena and Roman Reigns. My dad's favorite wrestler is Roman Reigns also. My dad and Danielle went to a WWE Live event. They promised to take me with them next time. I can't wait to go.

My favorite sport is baseball. My mom and I watch baseball on tv. I like to see the players hit home runs. I play baseball for the Little League RL3 and the Rockies. Coach put me in the outfield and on 3rd base, but I really want to be a pitcher or a catcher. My mom helped me find YouTube videos about baseball, so that I can be a better baseball player. When I am at home I practice pitching, catching, and throwing so that I can be a pitcher or a catcher soon.

What is your favorite sport? Why is that your favorite sport?

# FROM THE AUTHOR:

Thank you for reading my book.

**Jeremiah Jackson**

www.ingramcontent.com/pod-product-compliance
Lightning Source LLC
LaVergne TN
LVHW052303100826
845147LV00001B/126

* 9 7 8 1 9 3 6 8 6 7 9 4 3 *